AN AWFUL RACKET

Rita Ann Higgins was born in 1955 in Galway, Ireland, and still lives there. She published her first five collections with Salmon in Ireland, *Goddess & Witch* (1990), which combines *Goddess on the Mervue Bus* (1986) and *Witch in the Bushes* (1988), *Philomena's Revenge* (1992) and *Higher Purchase* (1996), followed by *Sunny Side Plucked: New & Selected Poems* (1996) and her latest collection *An Awful Racket* (2001) from Bloodaxe. Her plays include *Face Licker Come Home* (1991), *God of the Hatch Man* (1992), *Colie Lally Doesn't Live in a Bucket* (1993) and *Down All the Roundabouts* (1999).

She has edited *Out the Clara Road: The Offaly Anthology* and (with Gráinne Sweeney) *Word and Image: a collection of poems from Sunderland Women's Centre and Washington Bridge Centre.*

She was Galway County's Writer-in-Residence in 1987, Writer in Residence at the National University of Ireland, Galway, in 1994-95, and Writer in Residence for Offaly County Council in 1998-99. In October 2000 she was Green Honors Professor at Texas Christian University. Her many awards include a Peadar O'Donnell Award in 1989 and several Arts Council bursaries. *Sunny Side Plucked* was a Poetry Book Society Recommendation. She is a member of Aosdána.

ISBN: 1 85224 563 8

First published 2001 by
Bloodaxe Books Ltd,
Highgreen,
Tarset,
Northumberland NE48 1RP.

Bloodaxe Books Ltd acknowledges
the financial assistance of Northern Arts.

Cover printing by J. Thomson Colour Printers Ltd, Glasgow.

Printed in Great Britain by
Cromwell Press Ltd, Trowbridge, Wiltshire.

RITA ANN HIGGINS

An Awful Racket

BLOODAXE BOOKS

In memory of my nephew
Michael Mullins (Slim-2 Speed)
who died on 9th December 1999
aged 18 years and 11 months

Acknowledgements

Acknowledgements are due to the editors of the following publications in which some of these poems first appeared: *Descant* (USA), *Finger Post*, *A Fistful of Pens* (Derry), *Force 10*, *The Irish Times*, *Or Volge L'Anno / At The Year's Turning*, *Poetry Ireland Review*, *Poetry Review*, *Poetry Now*, *Ropes*, *The Shop*, *The South Carolina Review*, *Verse*, *The Whoseday Book* and *Women's Studies Review*.

Some of these poems have been broadcast by RTE radio and television and Lyric FM. The sequence 'The Jugglers' was especially written for National Women's Council of Ireland seminar *Out of Sight: The hidden poverty of women*; with special thanks to Cathleen O'Neill, whose 'Telling it as it is' case histories inspired this sequence.

'Mother and Son' is dedicated to Rod Stoneman, 'Why I Refuse To Be Gracious' to Lelia Doolan, and 'Our Brother the Pope' to Fr. Pat O'Brien.

Contents

Bare Bones

They called me mad.
and I called them mad
and damn them
they outvoted me.

NATHANIEL LEE

The house is topsy-turvy
with the painters
when they knuckle down
me and Lickspittle dislocate
(he's the cat)
his joints are in the hall
skull 'n' doss-bone
one or two on the stairs
(he's devil jointed)

Mine too are hither and thither
a few on the landing not moving
only good for tripping over and over
I tell a lie one dropped down and down
a heavy hoor nearly killing the meter man
who to give him his due never howled
he only went click, click, click.

Lickspittle's joints are here
miscellaneous splashes are there
I'm running scissor rings around the room
losing weight as I rotate.

If they move one more of my things
I'll make no bones about it
I'll tell the painters
(one of whom is my husband)

If you move one more of my things
you'll meet treble fibula with a scissor complex
and you'll go down and down
as true as mother is in her grave.

8

And you may not have
the meter man to break your fall
or give you his fountain due
and the only sound you'll hear
will be clack, clack, clack, everywhere.

The River

The shyness was painful,
before this not even the whisper
of a stolen kiss.

On the walk down towards the bridge
her head fitted his shoulder –
Gráinne's bed.

Wistful river
pulsating with greed
taking bits of everything
empty cigarette packets
(a lipstick wearer's handbag)
pieces of wood
her inhibitions.

Brazen sorcerer
never taking no for an answer,
all this slushing and gushing.

In no-time shyness slipped off her hips;
tonight she would wear lipstick
she would be young girl giddy
she would pirouette for nothing

she would show him her arse.

Soft as Putty

The judge stopped him going down
for clocking the bouncer
with a sock full of snooker ball.

His mother pleaded gentle jelly
wouldn't kill a fly boy
soft as putty, my Mickey.

Framed, she cried, framed,
'cos he looked grown up
with the lone eyebrow,
the sheared ear,
the ring in the lip,
the bottom lip,
wouldn't kill a maggot,
Mickey, my Mickey.

She told your honour, my honour
about how long her Mickey
would keep fifty wasps alive in a jar
before rolling them out
for the cat to curl
with his claw,
the claw of his left paw.

He could do community service –
he could work in an aviary,
he has a way with birds,
the gait of our canary;
he could work in a beeviary,
he has a way with bees.

My honour was impressed –
he said, clear the court,
clear it now, pretty please.

You'd Know He Had a Lovely Mother

He was in and out
of Madden's everyday,
always laughing.
He couldn't care less
about the weather,
or the tax on new shoes.

He spent hours
messing with the kids,
doing the three card trick,
blind man's bluff, ring-a-roses
or pin the tail.
He drove the dog up the walls
saying 'Where's the cat?'

He gave old Mrs Madden a hard time
about the artic licence she needed
for that wheelchair,
not to mention the brake fluid.
You're a right *scéiméir* was all she said,
as he spun her round the kitchen.

The bingo girls called him
'two little ducks'
on account of his arse
was so close to the ground.

He told them
if they weren't careful
he'd be the Clark Gable
to get into their knickers.
He'd give them clickety click all right.

They could shout check for a line across
but he was only scoring at the goal-post.
At this they howled,
blowing smoke in his face.

Then one day
before spring
he folded his clothes,
climbed the seventy-eight steps
to the tank near the reservoir
and flung himself in.

Three days later they found him
face down and dead.

After the funeral
Mrs Madden said,
you'd know he had a lovely mother
the way he folded them clothes.

Pater

I was
dodging him
for years.

Now he's dead
I'm dying
for his shadow

Mother and Son

(after Aleksander Sokurov)

I'd like to walk first,
let sleep be second;
let sleep always be second,
in fact let sleep be last.

It's very cold now mother,
when you wake up it will be warmer.
We can walk then to the postcard bench,
I'll read the years back to you.
I'll ask 'who was he' questions,
you'll pretend not to hear me.
I won't ever mind mother.

I want to walk but I have no clothes,
only that raincoat that smells of death.
How can I walk in a raincoat
that smells of death?

Listen to her, no clothes indeed,
what next I ask you?
We can keep ourselves to ourselves,
just you and me mother.
We don't need raincoats or people,
we can stay away from people.

I'll wrap a blanket round you
and carry you most of the way.
You, light as the air,
I'll hardly know I'm carrying you.

I'll know my gentle son,
I'll always know you are carrying me,
my bones will be breaking with pity.

For Crying Out Loud

(a response to Leopardi's 'The Calm After the Storm')

Listen Leo love,
pardon me for saying so
but that cockaleekie
about the storm
is hard to stomach.

A little less
of your lethargic lingo
would go a long way.

In other words Leo love
lighten up.

I'm no Prospero,
I'm the cabbage seller
and my study
is the streets.

A storm to you
is a drop in a bucket to me,
if I don't come out crying
I will end up eating cabbage,
my own cabbage
and nothing but cabbage

Nature is bounteous
when they buy my cabbage.
If I were to listen to you
you'd have me imagine
I sell my cabbage.

That's no good Leo love
live horse and you'll get grass
is up to snuff in airy fairy poems
but the cabbage seller must eat.
I have seven more
cabbage heads at home.

Anyway what storm were you on about?
I was there remember,
I felt no gust or gale,
storm in your head-cup was all.

If I feed them your theories
on what death heals us from,
on despair, on the misery of man,
they'd eat me alive
leaf by gangrenous leaf.

Anthem

Our fury was well invested
year in, year out.
I wouldn't give an inch,
you wouldn't give an inch.
Hammer and tongs our anthem.

On the morning you died
I could see no reason
to change the habits of a lifetime.

It was strange
saying the rosary round your bed –
half praying, half miming.
The room was cold
with that window open.
Some *piseog* or other was being acted out.
(Letting your spirit dander round Mervue.)

A half-smoked cigarette
lay nipped on your bedside locker,
no *piseog* here only you were probably dying for a drag;
your new fur-lined slippers in everyone's way,
you weren't planning to leave just yet.

The rosary was in full flight –
echoes of the old days
and every bit as long
half song, half whisper,
extra prayers for the devil knows what.

As far as I was concerned
you had died, end of story
end of our Trojan War.

Some nuisance more ancient
than your Conamara lingo
or the jagged stones of Inis Meáin
was playing puck with my sensible side,
the side I use for dancing,

making me for the smallest whisker of a second
want to tuck the blankets round you,
sparing you the waspish November chill.

Why I Refuse To Be Gracious

the hee-goat spleen rosteth, helpeth the coeliack
PLINY

My small intestine is anything but fine –
in fact my small intestine is anything but mine.
I have some of the most tangled and shrouded
reasons to whine, but do I ever, I never.

It's the gluten you see
and it hates the shite of me.
That jejunum the bugger
is the cause of all the trouble.
He does a handstand
when he sees a chocolate bar
or battered fish or battered chicken
or bread or cakes or custard creams.

When he's supposed to work
he'll throw a wobbler,
acts gimped or look inane
and carp and carp and malabsorb
until the stone of unripe grape
is portion plenty at the gate.

The inner circle talk now going round
is about the cleanest colon in town –
I'm pissed off it will never ever be me.

My mucosa makes the mosta
of my slighest little boasta
my villi is the dilli with the willi
in the middle of a field
each villus that should stand
just flops to beat the band
waiting myrtles and quinces
and shredded fifty pences.

My enterocytes acts the shitists
in the middle of the nightists
and the he-goat spleen
is nowhere to be seen
roasted or raw
or ready for the thaw
not a drop not a jigger
not a lick of the frigger
have I sampled since I was eighteen

The Chamber Pit

Through the chair Mayor
at the last meeting
or the meet before the estimates
I did propose that we congratulate
the man who put up the lovely crib.

I know I got a seconder,
I always get a seconder,
my proposals are legendary
for getting seconders,
but c'mere Mayor
through the chair
the trouble is
my proposal isn't here.

I'm not saying nothing
and this isn't a whine
only when a man
who's had as much tragedy
as the crib man
goes round and puts up a crib of that calibre
the least we can do
is the least we can do.

Not in any cap in hand way,
cribbers hate that malarky,
cribbers hate oligarchy,
it should come from
the pit of the councillors' chambers
which is often a snake pit
as we all know, ha ha.

Rumours about his wife
being a right dog in the manger
for running off with the coal man
just after he changed to Polish coal
are neither here nor there.

The crib man never complained
about her indiscretions before this,
when there was talk she did it with a bishop,
when anyone with half a brain knows
bishops don't do it for Christ's sake.

This carry-on is rumour heavy
and cropped up long before
the coal man started selling bottled gas on the side
(she always said he was a gas man).

Leaving aside bishops and gas bottles
the point is through the chair Mayor
that her cribbie sculpted the realest looking
baby Jesus and three of the wisest looking men
with duffle coats and slingback sandals
who looked like they came straight out of Galway Bay
on a wet day long before the Treatment plant
got the bum's rush.

I think we should be on the hands and knees
of this cribbie not to mind bothering
about the shadows in his wife's past.

Polish coal and Papal Nuncios
could never burn as bright
as the star he sculpted
out of that gone-off asbestos.

If we play our cards right this year
who knows next year
he might get the baby Jesus –
real looking as he is –
down off the lean-to roof
and land him in a bed of crisp dry straw.

Our Mothers Die On Days Like This

When there isn't a puff
and the walk from the bus stop
to the front door
isn't worth the longed-for
out-of-the-question cup of sweet tea
she can never have
because doctor do-little-or-nothing
told her face to face
it was the sugar or the clay
the choice was hers.

The choice was no choice
he knew it, she knew it.

When the heavy bill on the hall floor
with the final notice reminded her
once and for all she must turn out the lights,
her Angelus bell rang and rang.

The Weather Beaters

The bitter snap is over,
a few bones told them.
The two of them leg it
through the green
a hundred steps more or less
and the cure will be in hand.

The winter was too long,
this is the first bright day
and true to form
pep came back to step
it out across the Prairie,
the only open space in Castle Park.

They are not as old as they look,
these weather beaters,
karate-expert weather beaters,
they box it and kick it
with their falling off toes,
they shout while they do it,
one says the snow is an animal,
a pig-dog with warts the other says.

This bright day has given them hope,
antifreeze-cider-hope,
they're walking faster now,
they leg it across the green
faster than they did in ages.

The flea-infested couch they got
as a so-called Christmas present
can go to blazes,
they think this in unison
with their bachelor brains.

Today they stretch their bones,
their funny bones,
everything is funny today –
they say hello to two kids lighting a fire,
the kids say fuck off and die,
the weather beaters laugh and laugh.

The Fracture

The man in number seven
is waiting for God to call him.
He has lived long enough,
he has lived too long.

The worst thing is lighting the fires,
first in the kitchen then the sitting-room
same old ding dong.
Some days there is no draught
and when there is no draught there is no flame.

This day out of the deep blue
his thoughts seemed to cosy up to one another
they held a playful pattern, he was glad of it,
he would take their lead.

He brought the telly into the kitchen –
only thing is the kitchen has no comfortable chair.
After a lengthy battle on the rights and wrongs of it
a lone thought emerged, it told him what to do.

He dragged the armchair
from the front room to the back room
nicking his hip in the process.
(luckily it was his span new hip
not the other one, a feather fall would fracture)
The kitchen was too small
the kitchen table would have to go.

When herself was here
lighting the fires was a work of art
the tightly twisted paper first
the kippings he collected on their daily walks
the cinders from yesterday
the small coals on top
rising to a pyramid of love.
In no time they would interpret the sparks.

This day his thoughts were in a hurry
he held the reins long enough
he held the reins too long
the pattern was ravelled
the feather did fall.

He didn't like lighting fires
he didn't like eating off his lap
he didn't like the way the sunlight
crept into his kitchen in the mornings
and reminded him of things.

His world was tearing, the big split –
a sheet caught in barbed wire.
The kitchen table was out the back
the front room was now the back room
the kitchen was becoming the bedroom
upstairs was now downstairs.

Another lone thought prodded –
outside is not inside,
outside will always stay outside
out there will never get you in here
not today, not tomorrow
not the week after the races
not two weeks before Saint John's night.

That's right the old man reckoned
with a gush of youth in his veins
there is no why
there is no where
there is only out there
and it will stay out there
until the flames of hell smoulder and die.

Good Friday in Majorca

He said to her that morning,
this is going to be the day mama,
the day of all days.
No more Peach Schnapps in my porridge mama,
today Christ died for us,
today I will let people live,
and another thing mama –
this will be a free ride on my bus day.

He let everyone on his bus,
he let on their relations,
after that the people on the next street,
everyone on the next four streets;
he took no pesetas,
he spoke in sangria and sign
in, in, in, Schwein Hunde
and Wie Geht's your arse,
I love Jerusalem, get in, get in.

He let on all the grandfathers and grandmothers
and the great-grandmothers,
the place was crawling with great-grandmothers
and all the people he had met over the years
on his daily journey from Ar'enal to Palma.

He got all the grand people
and the great people to squash against the door,
some slid sideways to the ceiling,
the great-grandmothers were good at that,
he was pass remarkable about their knitting,
he said I hope you did not bring your knitting today
old mamas this is not a knitting day,
today we go to Palma to the procession.
He turned the air conditioning off,
he turned the loud music on –
soccer winning music,
Coppa Coblana stuff.

He didn't stop when the people pressed the bell,
red lights didn't matter or signs or arrows

or a million lemons,
in fact he gave the arrows the sign,
he gave the signs the finger, the middle finger,
he gave the lemons the bad eye –
'lemons lemons I see nothing but lemons'.
He told the people from Siesta Street to move back,
he abused them a bit, saying he had it from a good source
that they would sleep on knitting needles.
He warned them about harbouring chickens
under overcoats on Good Friday;
he said, them days are gone
this is Good Friday
not suckling pig Sunday –
we are going to market,
we are going to Palma to the procession,
enjoy the music.

After a while people thought
there might be an announcement –
the people were right,
once the rose window of La Seu Cathedral
came into view the bus driver said,

Amigos, today is Good Friday this is my bus –
you are getting a free ride all the way to Palma,
sit back on your neighbour,
get close to the one from the next street,
never you mind the crowd from Siesta Street,
they are all dreaming of roast suckling pig.
I have watched you over the years –
you are too standoffish,
squash in there; be in touch with your neighbour.
Christ died for you, you die a little today,
today is Good Friday, this is my bus
we go all the way to Palma.

A few grandfathers started to scream.
I knew it, I knew it, said the driver
I knew the grandfathers would be first to scream.
Shame on you old man
just because you are in your eighties
and people are sitting on your head –
look at that poor mama in the corner turning blue
do you hear her screaming?

I know you have a chicken inside that coat
because nobody could have a belly that size.

I knew the moment I saw you
you were the chicken hiding type,
you get a free ride all the way to Palma
and what do you do, you scream and whine,
you have two chickens inside your coat
I'm sure of it, you have it written all over your face.

Some brave grandmother plucked up the courage
to shout at the driver,
not the one going blue but a second cousin of hers
from Santa Ponsa up for the weekend.
Loco, she said, Loco.

The driver didn't like it,
he always said he hated back cheek from grandmothers
who had turning blue cousins up from Magalluf or Santa Ponsa.
Screams from chicken shitters would be one thing
but this was too much for him

Mama he said, this is Good Friday, this is my bus –
it may have a few dints from the narrow corners,
there may be a ladder swinging from the roof
where the painter tried to sneak on without paying,
if he had tried the front door like everyone else
he would know it was a no peseta day,
out of the goodness of my big heart
I bring you and half the neighbourhood
and their squakie kids
and grandfathers who think
I don't know the smell of chicken shit,
I bring you all to Palma
for the procession non-stop all the way
for no pesetas,
en route you see a million lemons
you bitter bastards,
I give you Copa Coblana loud as you like
and you call me loco
you said it twice
loco, you said, loco
mama are you crazy
get off my bus.

The Clemson Experience

*(Conference of Irish Studies. Conference centre
surrounded by golf course, formerly a plantation)*

In the Walker Golf Course where no one walked
Joyce's wet dreams were splashed about
in the name of the father.
Carson's bullets slip-jigged and reeled,
Yeats's black habits were boiled and peeled
more Joyce dot.com for psycho-netters –
Joyce in Celluloid, Joyce in hotpants,
Joyce in toilet with betters.

Heaney's bogmen were dragged up
by their rotting stubs,
their bones picked asunder,
the contents of their ancient bellies
made flesh and flung amongst us
on this golf course at Clemson, once a plantation
where tailgating is something dirty Yeats didn't do.

The golfers over-the-hilled it at 8 a.m.
in their twenties, in their trolleys, off their trolleys
on their starter's orders.

The man with the megaphone threw shapes.
'Proper golf attire does not include
grown men with big bellies prancing round
this 18 hole in suspender belts,
shorts should be of Bermuda persuasion
not to the shins or below
not too far above the knees,
no balls in the trees,
that last remark was a slip of the tongue.

Right you cock shots, you hot shots,
only collared shirts here,
shiftless losers over there,
no flashy ankle socks with tiger paws or other,
absolutely no swimwear, no Aran sweaters –
if you want Synge try Ballroom Four.'

Papers about what Jack B did to Lady G
while W.B. was exorcising his tea
or viewing *A Portrait* from his tightest orifice (with slides)
chaired by a Carolina Panther supporter from Chattanooga
or the pitying shape of Irish drama
as told through the space invaders in Friel's work
or learning the quotable Yeats and Heaney in three easy lessons
for after dinner speeches or the odd peace process.

Megaphoner-all-aloner was losing it with the golfers.

'Hey you, Mr Inappropriate chest of drawers
do you want me to send you in there
where they pick Heaney, poke Joyce,
pickle the bones from man of ice,
O.D. on Yeats and queer theory,
Tiresias and Art O'Leary.

Where all day is spent finding the missing link
between Behan, Boland and Lewinsky.
And you with the black leggings,
put your hand on your affliction
when I am dressing you down.

This is Clemson, home of The Clemson Tigers
where the Blue Ridge Mountains shield you
from the smell of that rotting cheese,
where Lake Heartwell ducks eat gluten-free bread,
where the azaleas and camellias
would sicken a sorry dog with that splash of colour,
where the chrysanthemums are edging in just for notice.

The choice is yours, will you wear proper golfing attire
or will I let the wind-filled professors at you?
Where they heaney time by plucking the maggots
and sucking the marrow out of the bones of the bogmen of Ireland
on this championship golf course, once a plantation.
What's it to be, you in the girl's knickers!'

They Always Get Curried Chips

Between her supermarket singsong
and the endless gossip she loves
Dolly's voice is nearly gone.

What scandal the builders throw her
is piffle, compared to when
the sisters-in-law come round.

Every extension is taken apart
brick by adulterous brick,
they know the footfall
and back-to-front baseball cap

of every builder who's doing it
with the wife's sister
or that skinny wan with the hippy hair,
they know him down to the birthmark
on his lovely arse.

They see the cracks in every
brick and mortar give-and-take
that was hammered out in back seats
below in condom alley valley,

where the hoods sell Ecstasy
and good for nothing cars
with nare a number plate
never mind a log book.

The extension is the thing –
they call it the granny flat,
it takes the harm out of it
like, one owner, mint condition
woman driver kind of shite.

It's not just small talk, it's all talk –
instead of good morning
it's good extension,
happy May day has become
happy granny flat day.

'She has three and a half kids and a lean-to'
(god bless the mark),
'my rafter's going up a Friday',
'my plumber is nearly upon me',
'my roofer is roofing like billy-o'.

Where will the big dogs go now
that's what I'd like to know
at the end of our row
there's one as big as a horse.

They keep him
and his four sets of teeth
in a back yard
full of broken busses and road signs,
the new extension will cover him,
an overcoat of concrete,
molar drive.

Dolly's new extension
will take your eye out,
it will have every doodad.
A couch that won't burn
no matter what
buttons that bring on the footstools,

a picture of a boy in blue
with a tear on his cheek,
a remote control
that dominates the curtains,
a dining-room table
that goes inside itself,
a grandfather clock that belts out rave
and Spanish sign language.

The extension means more than space,
her status will rise in the estate
so it was written on the bingo book.

The extension will tower above the hedge
the neighbours fashioned
to stop seeing Dolly
smoke a chunk of midweek.

As for the two-up and two-downers
she pities them, she'd tell you herself.
I pity them poor bastards
with nothing to show for themselves
only two-ups and two-downs.

Look at me, I could keep lodgers,
I could keep a small village in that granny flat
and still have room to spare
when the sisters-in-law come round.

And come round they do and often
they talk back-to-front-baseball caps
they talk shape, they talk size
when it comes to it
size is everything,
they talk backseat gobbledegook,
nothing is really sacred,

mind you they don't do politics or piss artists
but they do do priests, and how.
Tired of talking, it's time for food,

they always get curried chips,
they rarely get planning permission.

Snakes and Ladders

Deckie is out polishing the car again –
they think they got a great deal,
a great steal would be more like,
it's all paint and powder.

It was wrapped round a pole the other week,
the headlights doing buck and swing,
the chassis doing mime –
it's stitched together,
a goat in silk knickers.

Speedin down Claw Hammer Drive –
gadgets, geegaws, speakers,
Man United stickers,
furry things hanging from the dash,
the engine left sitting at the traffic lights.

Annie will bate seven shades out of him
give her anything but engines left sitting at traffic lights –
she wears the trousers in that house,
she wears the house in that trousers,
no sansculotte about that biddy,
she's trousered to the gills.

Deckie was shifted once
after she caught him shaggin' Picasso
she told him to wise up
and get the diesel out of his eyes.

The shagger still moults around
but the shaggin' is supposed to be done with
according to a local swing bag who doubles up
as a window leaner with a flair for
cock-cooling and garden gnome counselling.

But some of us plebs know better
when Deckie is at work
old Picasso acts the sidewinder
armed with his paintbrush
his bulging trousers,

he keeps his ladder in his underpants.

The Lads Said He Was a Sissy

He walks
up and down the green
with a bag full of stones
and his tiny dog –
the dog is always knackered,
you never saw such a pissed-off dog.

All day everyday,
walk walk bag of stones,
tired dog.

Some say he carries china
from the china factory
where he worked,
but it doesn't clink
and the struggle is too great,
it must be stones.

Years ago
he was a flasher,
he lived opposite our school.
At lunch time he would stand naked
in the window
and play with his genitals.

We're going to see the flasher,
'any takers' was the catch cry –
we went, we saw,
none of us said much
only, what's on him?
The lads said he was a sissy.

It broke the monotony
of who made the world
and why did she make the world?

He calls the dog Tartarus,
other times he called him
piss-head or come on wagon.

When Television came to Ballybrit
we were ready for it.

April Fool's Day in Jerusalem

The soldiers were everywhere –
running up and down steps,
in and out of this street,
this way that way zigzag way
around corners in their twenties.

I asked what was going on.
It's nothing, the man said,
they have to circumnavigate
and go through the streets,
and go through the houses,
they zigzag a little,
they up and down a little,
they around corners a lot,
it's nothing, enjoy the sunshine.

The Bag Boat

All's ya done was
went down in the morning,
put your back against the wall
and hoped that the stevedore
would give you the beck.

If he did
you navvied like the Firbolg
until the slings were full.

If forty bags a sling
was all they took,
you wouldn't give a damn
but you knew
you were giving more or less
than you would ever get back.

If one drop of rain fell
not one fertiliser bag
did you swing.

There was nothing for it
but jack up and go the pub.
One drop was an act of God,
two drops was a hurricane.

If you didn't get picked
you went home
taking misery with you,
of that you had a sackfull.

The ones with the docker's card
had it sewn up,
they were always picked,
hand picked, the cunts.

She Believed in Miracles

He was a painter
a house painter
he loved white
he wore white overalls
all the week,
overall he wore white
nice and tight
around the bum,
his car was white
his wife was white
she wore white ski pants
and a white tank top
she loved the tank top,
she loved the big top as well
but not as much as the tank top.

He told anyone who listened
that his mother was a falling down drunk,
he even told the priest Father Quirke.
Father father my mother
drinks herself under the table
every night, the white table.

Father Quirke didn't believe him
he knew that snowball's mother
was never in a pub in her life
the chemist shop now and again and again,
but never the pub
and if people don't see it
it doesn't happen.

At weekends Snowball liked to dress up –
his nice white slacks, a tasty white polo neck,
white gym shoes and crisp white sin free socks,
a key ring with a white rabbit dangling from it,
he never went anywhere without the key ring.

He told welfare
his mother had a drink problem,
he begged them for carer's assistance;
I'm a carer, he says, assist me
but they didn't believe him.

He didn't get much for painting houses,
he would only paint white –
if you wanted any other colour,
he said, sorry mam no can do,
he always said no can do.

His mother never went to the pub
in fact she didn't much like other people
unless they were wearing white
then she would say, loveen I like your tank top.
In fairness to her, she did like rabbits.

When she died
they found eight hundred
and forty-five empty cough bottles
in the coal bunker.

Snowball was grand first
then the bad dreams came
every snake-headed whipper snapper turned up.
The furies had a regular bus pass,
the minute his eyes closed they pounced
licking the soles of his feet
with their wirebrush tongues.

They told him to make a sculpture
out of the cough bottles for all to see
otherwise two of his flat feet
would never again do a soft shoe routine
while he pulled a rabbit out of a can of paint.

Give him anything but naked fear
he says, give me anything but naked fear.
He set the sculpture in the front garden,
it took the shape of a hippogriff
perched in a monkey puzzle tree.

People tried not to look at it
but it was there and it was big,
eight hundred and something cough bottles big.

They say it had a cure for bad chests
all you had to do was look at it
and you were phlegm free forever.
Wheezers were coming from all over Ireland,
a few from the outer Hebrides,
a bus load from Inverness,
there was talk of a crowd
of long term dope-smokers
up from Bengal Bay;
they were the real huffers and puffers,
more talk about eighteen Bedouins
from the Judaean desert
who tried the Dead Sea
but still they coughed.

People came and people looked –
one fat fella with a foul mouth
and a really chalky wheeze
said he was in for the long haul,
said he wouldn't go home till a miracle happened.
He got pneumonia and died.
His wife told the local paper she believed in miracles.

Lucky Mrs Higgins

When our mother
won a fridge
with Becker's Tea,
she got her photograph
in the *Sentinel*
shaking hands
with the man from head office.

The fridge was also
in the frame.
She wore a big wide hat
she kept on top of the wardrobe
for fridge winning days.

It went nice
with the crimplene two piece
she got for Mary Theresa's wedding.

In the photo
with the fridge
and the man from head office
she didn't look anything like herself.

Our Brother the Pope

Sorrow is better than laughter,
for by a sad countenance the heart is made better.
ECCLESIASTES

Few people know this
but Pope John the 23rd
was a member of our family.
His real name was
Pope John the 23rd Higgins.

He lived with us in Ballybrit,
I can't say he had his own room
but he didn't need it;
he had his own house,
our house.

He was there
when our father
brought home the mackerel,
when Yahweh Curran
whistled his way
round the twelve cottages.

He was there when we
painted the house
for the races
and when we
got the new range
Stanley the 9th.

When he died
nothing was the same.
The mackerel began to stink,
Yahweh Curran didn't whistle
for a solid month,
the picture show in Silk's Shed
was just a runaway wagon
with three wheels.

Our mother cried and cried.
Saint Jude and Saint Agnes
let her down big time,
as for poor Philomena,
she couldn't conjure up
a minor miracle if her life depended on it,
she was gone by the board.

The neighbours who were well clued in
queued up round the cottages
to offer their condolence,
they were soaking in grief.

We're sorry about the mackerel
they said one after the other,
holding their noses.
Our mother cried louder.

Hey Greggie

I didn't mind
sleeping in the shed,
it wasn't every night
for crying out loud,
only the nights
he had a skinful – bang.

I knew as true
as there's shit in a duck
that one day he'd get his –
and he did – quack.

He fell
and hit his head
off the garden wall – smack.

When he went down
he stayed down
big and all as he was – boing!

I'm still collecting his pension
and he's three years dead now.
I have lunch out
in the Imperial every week
and it's on him – clack.

The fall made a hole in his head,
a clean hole all things considered,
you'd fit a farmer's hand inside it – whack.

Every week in the Imperial
I drink to him –
I say, hey Greggie!
may you rot in hell-swell.

City Slicker

When Killer Kelly
drove past at speed
Mott the Hoople blazing,
with one hand out the window
holding the roof like a trophy
and Baby Keogh caught a glimpse
from the safer side of lace,
she thought for one split second
she could crush his lovely head with her thighs
and never throw any backwater priest the details
she knew the city had snaked into her veins.

My Face Goes Scarlet

*The only time kids these days went on their knees
is when they are giving blow jobs*

FR. JOHN KERRANE
Dunshaughlin, Co. Meath,
Irish Times, 4 December 1999

I'm sick of it
I've had it up to there.
They never stop
every night
its the same thing,
week in
week out.

They start hanging around the wall
in sixes and sevens,
if they're not smoking dope
they're sniffing glue.

And if they're not
sniffing glue
they're up the backs
giving blow-jobs.

And I wouldn't mind
some of them
wouldn't blow snow
off a rope.

My face goes scarlet
when I see them youngsters
on their knees.

I shout at them
I say, go on outa that, ye pups
but they're far too employed.

You know who I blame,
I blame the parents
for not wearing protection.

He Knows About Cars

The man with the greyhounds
knows about cars
though he never drove himself.
When he walks the dogs
he writes crime novels in his head.
When he hits a full stop you know it.
It's the chin, eyes and upper torso swing
that give him away.
The comma is more of a wobble than a fall.

On one leash he has six greyhounds,
on the other he has a light-hearted mongrel
whose feet hardly touch the ground.

She's a big jellyfish that one,
I have to bring her everywhere.
They'd eat her alive if I left her with them.
See that dint in her back,
they thought she was a hare once
and there was a quare hullabaloo,
skin and hair flying was nothing.

She's a great little watchdog though,
she hates the postman,
he knows too much for his small head –
he starts off about soccer
and he ends up
talking about stocks and shares
and Legionnaire's Disease,
on top of him being master mind
he's a scandal monger.

My neighbour was under the car one day
looking for his child's tooth
(the tooth fairy was a joy-rider).
The unwelcome soothsayer
with letters after his name
got down on his knees
and gawked in at him
that's how nosy we're talking.

The thing about cars is
when it's frosty
you should never
leave the wipers fifty fifty
'cos next morning
when you're turning her on
they'll snap
like a postman's knee.

The Sentence

Chatterina plucked pregnant pauses
out of the lips of good neighbours
and knitted them into
a thousand words per minute.

Himself measured words,
his phrases had short back and sides,
his verbs were anorexic
his nouns were Hail Holy Queens,
he mouthed the tight-rope of caution,
he was fond of the silent 'e'.

Chatterina was tell a tale and tell it well
and wrap it round a light-pole
and weave it up and down this estate
type of person. On top of that she was clean.

One day she was telling us about how
the Corporation tried to evict her
because she wasn't wearing the orange lipstick
set out in article two of the leasing agreement.

She was galloping to the finish line
with words jam packed with pig-eyed plurals and steam
when a frog got caught in her throat.

After the stroke
himself finished her sentence.

They Never Wear Coats

They start early on Friday night
in the girlfriend's house.
They pour into the new clothes
from Fenwicks
or the bargain rail.

These tubes on legs,
high heels on stilts,
will paint the town red.
A swig for you,
a swig for me –
'that looks lovely on ya hinny,
I'd nearly do ya meself.'

With perfect Revlon faces
they hit Newcastle
linking each other
six or seven across.
Close enough to trade
secret for Geordie secret.

When eleven comes
they fall from grace
onto the night club queue.
Carol as always has to pee,
'Have ya had a good look like,
I'll shove yer face in it for ya?'

More laughter, eye contact is made
the bonding started long before this
in another pub in the Bigg Market.
A glance that lingers longer than a second
is at least the promise of a blow job.

They look like models,
same shakey walk,
same knicker jaw-line,
they never wear coats.

The bouncers can look all they like
through their gable-end shoulders.
They have close shaves,
they have no necks,
they list on the soles of their feet,
a practised technique.
They say one of them done it for a week
without blinking.
The money raised went to
the battered bouncers ball.

In the lane
near Tyneside Cinema
earlier glances are being metamorphosed.
Shadows fumble, they nearly fall
with heart-stopping ticks of lust.

They know the words of all the songs,
they sing them all day in the workplace.
'I try to say goodbye and I choke.
I try to walk away and I stumble.'
This night they sing louder
helped by vodka and gin.

Again they link their precious friends,
they are ready for Geordie,
no need to beat around the bush,
they speak his language.

'I'll shag him the neet
and he won't know what hit him,
big Geordie fuck.'

The Visionary

The woman in the sweet shop
is turning into her mother.
Only the other week
she was young
when talk of weddings,
wallpaper, new fridges
and a small flat in the town was all talk.

Then for God knows why
he took a bus that never stopped
and she was left
with the wallpaper shame
of not having any fruit in her womb
that she might buy
white socks for.

Her mother's tiredness
grew into her,
her mannerisms,
her thanks be to Gods.

When she totted up the numbers
she wore her mother's glasses.
She joked about it,

'Sure what difference does it make
haven't me and mammy
the same vision anyway,
aren't we both far sighted?'

An Awful Racket

In the winter
we don't light a fire everyday,
three days a week max
always on a Saturday night though.

Me and the kids sit around the fire
and sing songs, the twins clap,
they play Baker's Man
we have great craic,
except for Justin
I nearly had him in a taxi
that's why we called him Justin.

He's fourteen now, he's always angry.
'What good is looking into the fire like spas,
what's fuckin wrong with ye?' he says.

Then all hell breaks loose.
I don't allow fowl language,
I didn't bring them up like that,
then the twins start bawling
and I can't shut them up.
The eldest starts first,
he was born ten seconds before Paul.
I say to Peter, 'If you don't shut that
fucking cake hole, I'll throttle ya.'
Then Paul starts,
he has lungs like a broken exhaust.

Last year when things
were a bit slack
we burned their father's wardrobe.
We split up two years ago,
we parted on amiable grounds though.
I couldn't aim
And he couldn't miss.

The kids thought it was a howl
me taking a hatchet to the wardrobe
on Christmas Day.

There was nothing much in it anyway,
only a couple of his shirts
I'd forgotten to put in the mincer,
old papers where the cat had kittens
and a banjaxed tennis racket.

That racket caused more trouble;
one day no one wanted it,
the next day they all wanted it.
I ended up throwing it on the fire.

It crackled like lard.

Succubus and Her Sisters

I haven't a hope in hell against Succubus
who comes to you in deep slumber
with her dying-for-it phantom sisters,
their bala-kelpie cleavage,
their coal-bucket eyes,
they dance around your bed
letting on to be rancour free, bereft of bile.

Just when you thought it was safe
to take a loving astral leap in my direction
another gang of shadowy nebulas
beckon to the goblins in malevolent hot-pants
who lurk on your landing
waiting to slither under your duvet
to hammer out ghoulish acts
unheard of in any ancient Sanskrit,

they leave you drained,
they don't leave you dry.

Black Dog in My Docs Day

Your mother rings from your grave.
I say where are you?
She says, I'm at Michael's grave
and it looks lovely today.

Duffy misses you,
Jennifer Lydon misses you.
You were grand until depression
slipped into your shoes –
after that you dragged your feet
big long giraffe strides. Slim-2 Speed.

When depression slept
you were up for anything,
go for it and you went for it –
times you got it, other times you lost it,
you didn't play the lyre,
you played the horses,
lady luck was often with you
you never looked back
William and Lara miss you.

When you were a few months old
I went to see you in hospital,
you had meningitis.
The nurse told me that I had to leave,
I told her you were my nephew,
she said you still had meningitis.
You had days months and years to go,
the crowd in Maxwell's miss you.

When your mother said,
Michael started school today
I thought you were too young,
you grew up without telling us,
you went to sleep small,
when you got up
you were kitchen-table tall,
you had fourteen years to go.

A messer in your Communion photos,
leaning against the wall in hidden valley
arms akimbo, one foot behind the other,
you were ready to trip the light fantastic
the body of Christ.

Odd times in Castle Park
when you were passing the house,
I'd said, Michael wait up
you'd say, no way José!
I've got the black dog in my shoes
I have to drag him half way across Ireland ,
I have to do it today and it must be raining.

Our Jennifer misses you
Christy misses the long chats with you,
he wished you didn't talk so much in the bookies,
Heather misses you,
Larry didn't know you
but Larry misses you because Heather misses you.

Eleven years to go you dyed your hair,
your uncles didn't know you,
they didn't know what they were missing.
No school wanted you.
You wanted Nirvana, you wanted The Doors,
you wanted shoes you didn't have to drag
you wanted hush puppies or Gandhi's flip-flops
instead you got Docs with a difference
the joy-roy gang miss you.

For your Confirmation
you took Hercules as your middle name,
you wanted a sweatshirt and baggy pants,
you left your mother and George at the church,
kiss me there you said to your mother
pointing to your cheek
and you were off with your friends,
soldier of Christ.
Auntie Mary and Aidan miss you,
Johnny misses you,
Caroline Keady misses you.

Móinín na gCiseach Tech said you failed maths,
you went in yourself to set the record straight.
Your mother has the letter of apology the school sent.
No school wanted the boy with blue hair
Dana C. and Caroline L. miss you.

You did the junior cert
with 'Dóchas an Oige',
we went down on open day,
you made us cranky buns,
real conversation stoppers.
Bobby and Shane miss you.

The day you and I filled in
your passport application
your shoes were empty
except for your long dreamy feet,
they matched your fanciful answers.
Name: Michael drop-dead-gorgeous Mullins.
Who do you want to be when you grow up?
A rolling fucking stone baby
Keith The Buckfast Kid misses you,
Margaret and John miss you.

The black dog came and went,
he didn't answer to Lassie
but when you said, hey Cerberus!
an idiotic grin came over his dogface.
The tea-leaf who just got out misses you.

When I visited you in the Psych first
you were outside sitting next to
a bucketful of cigarette ends.
I said you'd need to cut down
on the fags or you'd end up killing yourself.
We laughed till we nearly cried.
Granny Bernie misses you
Alice and Brendan miss you
you had a year left give or take.

You talked a lot about your daughter Erin,
she was eighteen months you were eighteen years.
You were here she was over there.
You called to Father Frankie
and asked if one day you could have Erin baptised,
you were soaking to the skin that day,
you were always walking in the rain,
docs filled with despair day,
black dog in my docs day.
Jackie from the psych misses you.

The day you got out for the last time
you and I walked from our house to Carnmore.
We had a drink at the crossroads
You weren't supposed to with the medication.
Fuck it you said if all those smarties I took
didn't kill me a pint of pissie beer hardly will.

You showed me round the house,
you said it was spooky
and if you were going to top yourself
it would be here you'd do it, and you did.
Auntie Carmel in Florida misses you,
Jennifer said you had a girlfriend,
Linda misses you,
Claire from Waterside House misses you.

You wanted to fathom the world
but your legs were tired,
you had two months left.
Cookie and Jillian miss you.
You talked about the dark hole
you often found yourself in,
you were happy when you got out
but when you were in it,
there was no talking to you,
you had weeks to go.
The Rinnmore gang miss you.

You got a bad 'flu
and the 'flu got you
the Millennium Bug,
your days were numbered.

Depression and the 'flu didn't travel
but you did and you never came back.
On December the 9th 1999
you hanged yourself.
Paddy L. and Michael Flaherty miss you.

Your mother rings from your grave
I say where are you?
She says, I'm at Michael's grave
and it looks lovely today.

They Never Clapped

(after Sirkka-Liisa Konttinen)

Valerie

She was two the first time she came,
she cried and cried.
I told her mother
you're wasting my time and your money,
she's a crier not a dancer.
She dances at home the mother said.
Well let her stay at home I said,
I took no guff off them
at two or twenty.

Lily

She did 'Sugar Plum Fairy'.
She got ninety seven out of a hundred,
ashen little pus on her.
She was bawling in her sleep,
she had the runs all morning,
but ninety-seven out of a hundred
not bad for three-and-a-half.

Dolly

When I see her dancing there
I see me dancing there;
when people admire her
they admire me.
We live through our daughters,
everyone knows that.
After seven kids
I'm coming back to it,
I'll look the spit out of her
only older.
When the mothers go for bronze
I'll get it I know I will.
It's just my outlook on things.

Dolores

She gets all her notions
from the telly that one,
she'd make a smashing child model
so finicky about her appearance
when she wears a dress for a couple of hours
she throws it in the wash basket,
this goes on all day every day.
On top of all that she'll only wear pink.
When I look in the laundry cupboard
and the washing is piled ten foot high
and it takes me four hours to iron it
I know I've trained her well.

Carol

One of them is getting married on me,
she's pregnant by a married man
after all the money I spent on dancing lessons.
She is not marrying him thank God,
he's not worth it she says.
She wants to take my three-piece suite,
mind you she's only going round the corner.
I suppose I could sit on it in her house.
It wouldn't be the same though, would it?

Sally

She could dance before she could walk,
we'd tie her to the back of the door on a pair of reins
and let her find her feet, she loved it.
Only problem was when you were having
a cup of tea you'd have to watch it,
nine times out of ten a leg would swing up,
my big hope was that one day
the two legs would work together
and she would make us proud
me and her father.

Sonya

My lass had a chance
to do a part in Les Mis,
in London if you don't mind.
My neighbour says London how are ya?
She had an ear infection
the day of the audition.
I don't know about London
she dances on my tips here.
I'd have to be making awful big tips
if she was dancing in London.
After me and her father split up
the tips was everything
I told her straight to her face,
I said, Sonya love
my tips is all we've got.

Florrie

The girls are measured every year,
if they don't grow at the right rate
they are out on their ear.
I always whisper to my lassie
when I'm tucking her in
mirror mirror on the wall
mirror mirror make her tall.
It's not their fault if they don't grow
and you tell them that,
you say it's not your fault if you don't grow,
at the same time you watch them
out of the corner of your eye.

Rosie

The careers officer
called her an 'Outdoor girl',
she liked it, it sounded kind of dirty.
He said he'd bet she could dance
up the butter queue and not be out of breath.

She asked him in her best dancing accent
how long was the butter queue,
he told her straight up
three quarters of a man-made mile.

Kelly

Her grandfather
sews all her dancing costumes
he's seventy, she's the apple of his eye.
All she does is wrap her legs
the wrong way round a chair,
drop her head forward,
peep out from behind her hair
in a certain way,
show him how she can lick her bottom lip
over and over
and he sews like billy-o.

Annie

Eventually she had to get a right job
with her brains and all.
She was fifth in charge
in a psychiatric ward.
Late at night in her leotards
(which were done to death in rhinestones)
she practised for the patients,
she did them ballroom and tap the odd tango,
they never clapped.

The Jugglers

1 *The Jugglers*

The Corpo bunged us all together
as part of some high and mighty pilot project,
it's high and mighty all right
but the lifts don't work.

The gangs know we are all lone parents,
they give you a cold stare
scares me to death but I never let on,
you have to act tough,
you have to grow a second skin;
mine's a tiger skin,
I wear it everywhere,
when I pass the druggies on the stairs
I growl, I make like I'm vicious,
I have to otherwise you're fair game.

The guys storing stolen property are just as bad,
they whizz by you at break-neck speed,
they'd knock you down as quick as they'd look at you;
when you pass them you give them a look that says
if you interfere with me or my kids
I'll kick the shite out of you.
Otherwise they'd have you hiding
Shergar's head in your chest of drawers.
This place is no great shakes to live in
but it's all we've got.
The dealers call it Bastards Bush.

I say to the kids, don't look at anything
on the way down those stairs;
the kids say to me like parrots,
we didn't look at anything mam,
we didn't look at the needles
or the shit or the broken glass.

Sometimes when I'm safe in my own flat
with all the locks and bolts on
I forget to take off the tiger skin.
The kids say, Mammy why are you cross again today?

The kids want the food they see on telly.
I say telly isn't real,
when the ads are on I turn the telly off,
mind you it's wearing me out.
Tanya says mammies on the telly are nicer than me
even though she's only four
I feel hurt, I know I'm too hard on them.
I have to watch the food,
I'm on food patrol
and when they bring their friends in
I have to say spare the bread,
it kills me to have to say that to them.
it makes me feel mean.

I'm a Stretcher.
I can stretch things,
I crumble up one and a half Weetabix
and pretend they are getting two;
I add water to the milk,
they never know.
I never seem to say anything but
who was at the fridge
and who drank the last drop of milk,
I hate myself for it.

My neighbour and me meet every Friday night
we go shopping for bargains together,
we save pennies here and there
on overripe fruit and dodgy vegetables
after sell by date stuff.
We hang around the shops until closing time.
If there are any cooked chickens left
we get them at half price.
Our Dylan says our Saturday dinners
are nicer than our Sunday dinners;
we have chicken on Saturday
and soup on Sunday.
He says his friend Billy has roast on Sunday.
I say he's a liar, I bite my lip.

3 *If Looks Could kill*

We all hate the moneylenders
but we need them for the Communion gear and that
it's the only time our families get together, barring funerals,
and I wouldn't give to show
that my girls won't look their best
even if I'm paying for it for two years.
One day Catherine from the corner house said,
I suppose the moneylenders have to live too.
We just looked at her.

4 *The Clinic*

I went up for help
with the shoes and uniforms,
that sort of thing.
The woman at the hatch was a right fuckin wagon,
she said I was in the wrong place.
It took me two buses to get there.
I asked her where was the right place.
Try the Vincent de Paul, she said.
When I got outside
I cried with rage.

5 *Christmas*

Two weeks before and two weeks after Christmas
I don't give the bill boys anything,
I stock up for the Christmas.
Any money I have goes on things for the kids.
I make sure they have a good Christmas,
we even have Christmas cake.
The funny thing is the kids don't like Christmas cake.

January and February are very bleak.
I owe everyone and they are not shy about telling me.
My nerves always get the better of me,
the doctor says I should take something
to calm me down, I'm highly strung.
When a car pulls up with a zero zero number plate
I know its someone looking for money.

I say to the doctor I'd rather live on my nerves
than take anything, then by early February
I go back and ask him for something,
something small to tide me over.

6 *Queuing*

You think queuing for food is bad
but queuing for a hospital appointment is worse,
at least you know what a loaf of bread is,
you don't know what they are saying up here –
they look down on you like you were shit,
they use another language,
a keep them guessing language,
a language never heard up our side
and I've heard some choice language believe you me.
They might be educated
but they're just as intimidating as the pushers.
You go in feeling bad,
you come out feeling worse.

70

If I won the Lotto
I'd get a headstone for Anto's grave.
He died young,
he didn't just burn the candle at both ends,
he ate the candle.
I wouldn't say it was the drink killed him
but it wasn't the milk either.
He was a good father though,
the kids loved him.

When he died the neighbours made a collection.
A good neighbour round here
is when they know every detail about you
and they still like you.
They like me more than I like me
'cos I don't like me at all.

I'd probably take the kids to Blackpool
I saw it on Coronation Street once
it had lots of rides and games for the kids.
I'd buy them new toothbrushes
they have the same ones for years.

I'd buy lampshades for all the bulbs,
It's just one of those things
you put on the back boiler like a piano
or a Triton shower.
Lampshades were never a priority
in this house.